# THIS NOTEBOOK BELONGS TO:

_______________________________

Made in the USA
Middletown, DE
14 March 2023

26780620R00061